INTERPRETING
ASTROLOGY

CHRIS MARSHALL

Published in 2002 by Caxton Editions
20 Bloomsbury Street
London WC1B 3JH
a member of the Caxton Publishing Group

Designed and produced for Caxton Editions
by Open Door Limited
Rutland, United Kingdom

Editing: Mary Morton
Typesetting: Jane Booth
Digital imagery © 2002 Photodisc Inc.

Title: Interpreting Astrology
ISBN: 1 84067 301 X

INTERPRETING
ASTROLOGY

CHRIS MARSHALL

CAXTON EDITIONS

CONTENTS

CONTENTS

Far right: different cultures in different periods of human history have developed their own astrological systems.

Below: the entire universe is composed of many different frequencies of energy in constant motion.

INTRODUCTION

Astrology is the oldest of all the ancient sciences. It has been used throughout recorded history and in every civilisation and culture as a means of helping people understand the forces at work around them and within themselves. It enables a person to recognise that they are not an isolated being but an important, if small, part of that much larger being which is the very universe itself. The entire body of the universe is composed of many different frequencies of energy in constant motion. As these energies stream across the universe in different combinations, they form into patterns that can be as large as a star or as small as a human being or as infinitesimal as an atom. Astrology studies how these energy streams interact. Therefore, astrology can be defined as the science of relationships.

No matter how useful and ancient astrology is it is still not yet a complete science. Different cultures in different periods of human history have developed their own astrological systems dependent on the needs of their particular culture and the knowledge of the solar system available to them. But, as history often shows us, just as new information can be learned, old information can also be forgotten. As such, a modern astrological system incorporating the latest scientific discoveries is not necessarily better or more accurate than one used thousands of years ago. There is still so much we have yet to learn about the workings of our solar system even in our technological age. But there is no doubt that this knowledge will be incorporated into the astrological system in the fullness of time.

This book focuses on traditional Western world astrology that has the Sun as the main point of reference. The interpretations are not dissimilar from the classical teachings used by the ancient Greeks although the three outer planets Uranus, Neptune and Pluto, which were discovered in more recent centuries, are also included.

THE CONSTELLATIONS

When we look up at the night sky, there are many groupings of stars visible in every direction. Ancient civilizations associated these groupings, or constellations, with the mythological gods and goddesses in their religious and philosophical systems. The names for the constellations were not chosen arbitrarily. The constellation of Virgo which has the symbol of the virgin carrying sheaths of newly harvested wheat, is most prominent in the night sky at the end of Summer when the time is ripe to bring in the harvest. A study of classical mythology reveals the reasons for how each constellation derived its name.

Right: the constellation of Virgo which has the symbol of the virgin carrying sheaths of newly harvested wheat, is most prominent in the night sky at the end of Summer.

Far right: when viewed from the Earth, the Sun during the course of one year appears to travel through a circular band of the sky of about 18 degrees of latitude.

There are many constellations, but only 12 of them compose our Zodiac. When viewed from the Earth, the Sun during the course of one year appears to travel through a circular band of the sky of about 18 degrees of latitude. This band of sky encompasses a narrow circle of constellations around the Earth through which the Sun apparently passes. This group of constellations is known as the ecliptic. The 12 Zodiac signs represent the constellations the Sun appears to journey through each year. The following section describes the characteristics of each of the 12 Zodiac signs.

Above: Aries symbolises new life, new beginnings and the impulse to create.

ARIES

DATES:	March 21st– April 19th
TEMPERAMENT:	Extrovert
RULING PLANET:	Mars
ELEMENT:	Fire
QUALITY:	Cardinal
AREA OF THE BODY:	Head

Aries is the first sign of the Zodiac. Extending over the Spring period, it symbolises new life, new beginnings and the impulse to create. The symbol of Aries is the ram that will fight to be the first and refuse to back down. People born under this powerful sign are aggressive and assertive not so much because they want to control others, but rather because they have an almost childlike enthusiasm for life and will not accept any kind of restraint. Ariens possess tremendous reservoirs of courage and self-belief. They initiate new activities independently and without hesitation, however impulsive or foolish this may seem to others. Impatience makes it hard for Ariens to look before they leap! They are too competitive to take advice or share and for this reason they often find themselves in confrontational situations.

Sometimes, Ariens can put so much energy into initiating schemes that they often run out of steam before the goal is attained. This leaves the door wide open for other, more measured, Zodiac signs to pick up from where Aries left off and so the final credit for success can go elsewhere.

Being involved with an Aries is sure to be a memorable, whirlwind experience although Aries' lack of sensitivity to the feelings of others will lead to turbulent periods. But once they learn a little diplomacy and gain the patience to follow projects through to completion, Ariens always achieve a great deal.

TAURUS

DATES:	April 20th– May 20th
TEMPERAMENT:	Introvert
RULING PLANET:	Venus
ELEMENT:	Earth
QUALITY:	Fixed
AREA OF THE BODY:	Neck and throat

Each Zodiac sign balances the extreme traits of the previous sign. In this case, whereas Aries was impulsive and confrontational, Taurus by contrast is steady and patient. This is not to suggest that Taurus lacks ambition – far from it. In fact, Taurus is better equipped to accumulate money and possessions than any other Zodiac sign! The symbol of Taurus is the bull that unwaveringly treads the traditional furrows of life in the absolute certainty that material success will eventually be secured. The Taurean person is not particularly introspective or an original thinker.

Rather, Taureans instinctively understand that money is a practical necessity in a physical world to buy the lifestyle they desire. Their love of comfort and opulent surroundings can be indulgent, but Taureans only feel emotionally secure once they have all their treasured possessions around them. The Taurean appreciation for beauty is highly developed. They make great efforts to improve their appearance and respect others who do the same. To those they love, Taureans are generous, loyal, very warm and sensual. However, the desire to completely possess what is loved means that Taureans can be stiflingly possessive in close relationships and annoyingly stubborn when challenged. Sexual jealousy is a particular danger. Taureans are slow to anger, but – be warned – they have an explosive and long-lasting temper when eventually roused!

Below: their love of comfort and opulent surroundings can be indulgent, but Taureans only feel emotionally secure once they have all their treasured possessions around them.

GEMINI

Below: the person born under the sign of Gemini is mentally inclined to scholarship and has a greater need than most to get a good education.

DATES:	May 21st– June 21st
TEMPERAMENT:	Extrovert
RULING PLANET:	Mercury
ELEMENT:	Air
QUALITY:	Mutable
AREA OF THE BODY:	Shoulders and arms

every idea will always evoke an opposite point of view: this is the basis of intellectual debate. The person born under the sign of Gemini is mentally inclined to scholarship and has a greater need than most to get a good education.

Always curious about the world and other people, Geminis love travel, varied company and witty repartee. Their easy-going charm and inventive ideas make Geminis popular and welcome at any social gathering. Geminis are truly original thinkers and can always be relied upon to give a unique slant to any conversation. Idle gossip can pose a danger, however. Their ability to use words creatively makes Geminis great writers and teachers. It also helps them talk their way out of many awkward situations! There is a very cunning side to the Gemini mind. It would be wrong to assume that because Geminis are intellectual they lack emotion. In fact, much of what appears to be a Gemini's reasoned opinion is simply based on how they feel at that particular moment. The duality of Gemini runs deep. Geminis do not need material possessions to feel secure, but must occupy their minds to avoid nervous tension. Any involvement with a typically non-conformist Gemini will be a lively and contradictory experience!

The symbol for Gemini is the Twins representing the two pillars of knowledge with the gateway of wisdom between them. The intellectual Gemini, more than any other sign of the Zodiac, expresses the duality of thought. Thought by its very nature is twofold because

Cancer

DATES:	June 22nd–July 22nd
TEMPERAMENT:	Introvert
RULING PLANET:	Moon
ELEMENT:	Water
QUALITY:	Cardinal
AREA OF THE BODY:	Chest and digestive organs

Cancer is ruled by the Moon and as such it represents our connection with the past, both on an individual level through the subconscious and on a collective level through family and heritage. The symbol is of the crab that has a tough outer layer of armour to protect the great vulnerability inside. Though people born under the sensitive sign of Cancer appear resilient and can be shrewd in business, they are in fact extremely shy and afraid of being ridiculed. Cancereans rarely laugh at themselves and are physically delicate when under stress. When threatened, Cancereans withdraw into solitude even though their instinct is to reach out for comfort.

They are very difficult for other people to predict because their moods change so quickly. Cancereans can fluctuate between cheerful optimism and withdrawn melancholia with disorientating speed. The hub of the Cancerean's universe is the home and family on whom they readily lavish their maternal and nurturing love. This might sometimes feel smothering to more independent signs, but the genuine compassion and sympathy that Cancereans radiate will always win them support. Cancereans are not particularly materialistic, but the fear of suffering any kind of discomfort makes them cautious and careful with their money. They are responsible to employers and excel in work situations where they can harness their boundless imagination and emotional depth.

Below: Cancereans are responsible to employers and excel in work situations where they can harness their boundless imagination and emotional depth.

Below: Leos really shine in social situations and their infectious enthusiasm makes them the life and soul of any party.

LEO

DATES:	July 23rd–August 22nd
TEMPERAMENT:	Extrovert
RULING PLANET:	Sun
ELEMENT:	Fire
QUALITY:	Fixed
AREA OF THE BODY:	Heart and upper back

Leo is ruled by the Sun, that star at the centre of our solar system which provides life-giving light and warmth to everything around it. This majestic power is reflected in the regal lion that is the symbol for Leo. People born under the sign of Leo are flamboyant characters who bestow a magnanimous generosity on everyone around them and certainly know how to have fun! Time, attention, money or anything else is there to be shared. All Leos expect in return is to be the centre of attention. They hate being ignored or challenged in any way. Leos really shine in social situations and their infectious enthusiasm makes them the life and soul of any party. They make passionate lovers and are very loyal to friends and lovers alike. This self-assured exuberance means Leos work hard in professions where they can be noticed and appreciated for their creative input. High-profile careers such as acting suit them well. But in any field, Leos like to be the boss and are not so comfortable in subordinate positions. There is a fine line between Leos' dramatic self-confidence and their tendency to be overbearing which means diplomacy is not a strong point. Pride can be a problem, but others make allowances for Leos because it is clear that Leos can be relied upon to give all of their time and considerable enthusiasm to any project they feel is worth the effort. Personal integrity is very important to sincere Leos.

VIRGO

DATES:	August 23rd–September 22nd
TEMPERAMENT:	Introvert
RULING PLANET:	Mercury
ELEMENT:	Earth
QUALITY:	Mutable
AREA OF THE BODY:	Intestines and abdomen

Virgo, or the Virgin, represents purity of thought. The symbol shows a virgin woman carrying freshly harvested sheaths of wheat. The period of Virgo coincides with the ending of Summer and the bringing in of the harvest. The harvest that the Virgo-born person reaps is the wisdom grown out of long experience. Nothing is more important to Virgo than the power of the mind and much time is spent gathering as wide a range of knowledge as possible to avoid being caught short or lacking in some vital piece of information. Much of life revolves around work because to a Virgo, life means mental activity. Here they must learn the important truth that the mind is a good servant but a poor master. Not everything in life can be reduced to a set of facts. However, Virgos' meticulous precision and efficiency makes them valuable workers, though their habit of focusing in on fine details can be an irritation to people! What others often fail to recognise is that, however critical Virgos seem, they are invariably far harder on themselves. This capacity for critical discrimination gives Virgos an astute insight into matters

Below: their capacity for critical discrimination gives Virgo an astute insight into matters concerning health and they can become great healers.

concerning health and they can become great healers.
This sensitivity means they must avoid food when under stress as their digestive system can be easily disrupted. Contrary to popular opinion, Virgos are not indifferent to sexual adventures but, as in everything else, quality is more important than quantity!

Below: people born under the sign of Libra strive for harmony in all things. Diplomats to the last. Work in public relations, the law or arbitration suits them well.

LIBRA

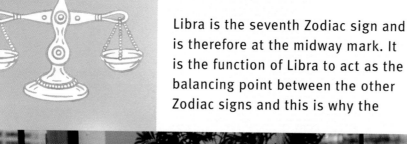

DATES:	September 23rd–October 22nd
TEMPERAMENT:	Extrovert
RULING PLANET:	Venus
ELEMENT:	Air
QUALITY:	Cardinal
AREA OF THE BODY:	Kidneys, lower back and buttocks

Libra is the seventh Zodiac sign and is therefore at the midway mark. It is the function of Libra to act as the balancing point between the other Zodiac signs and this is why the symbol for Libra is a pair of scales. People born under the sign of Libra strive for harmony in all things. Diplomats to the last, Librans seemingly are unable to make up their minds about anything. They are charming and sociable people who hate being alone. They need to work in partnership with others and are constantly seeking someone to unite forces with. Love is very important to Librans and they generally feel incomplete until they are married or have made a commitment. The danger for them is becoming too involved with someone too soon. Because of their fear of being alone, they are often tempted to stay in an unhappy relationship far longer than they should. But in reality, Librans are so easy-going and flirtatious that those who settle later in life will have had ample opportunities for love en route! Friendships are also important because Librans constantly need the approval and companionship of others. Despite what is often said, Librans are not lazy, but they are sometimes slow to find their feet. They often do not feel really in control of their lives until after their 30th birthday. Work in public relations, the law or arbitration suits them well. Librans are also very creative people and often gravitate to the performing arts and music.

SCORPIO

DATES:	October 23rd–November 21st
TEMPERAMENT:	Introvert
RULING PLANET:	Mars / Pluto
ELEMENT:	Water
QUALITY:	Fixed
AREA OF THE BODY:	Bladder and sex organs

Libra, the previous sign, is known as the balance. On one side of that balance is Virgo, representing pure clarity of thought. Here on the other side is Scorpio, which embodies the whirlwind of emotional intensity. The symbol for Scorpio is the scorpion with the legendary sting in its tail. People born under the sign of Scorpio are intensely passionate about everything they do. They are also very secretive and rarely trust anyone enough to reveal their full agenda. Love and particularly sexual passion are a constant obsession for Scorpios and anyone having a relationship with one is unlikely to forget about it! Although they make great lovers, Scorpios are possessive and relentlessly competitive. They tend to see sex as an expression of power. This can easily lead to jealousy and thoughts of revenge. This is where the scorpion's sting is likely to appear. Scorpios' temper is explosive and they do bear grudges. Much of a Scorpio's life involves learning to control their overwhelming desires through creative willpower. They are also fascinated by ultimate life and death questions. Scorpios' ability to look beneath the surface of things makes them particularly good at psychology. They also excel in fields such as investigative journalism or anything that requires secrecy and stealth. Whatever or whoever they become involved with, Scorpios would rather die than back down.

Above: although they make great lovers, Scorpios are possessive and relentlessly competitive.

Above: Sagittarians love to broaden their horizons constantly through travel or study.

SAGITTARIUS

DATES:	November 22nd– December 21st
TEMPERAMENT:	Extrovert
RULING PLANET:	Jupiter
ELEMENT:	Fire
QUALITY:	Mutable
AREA OF THE BODY:	Hips and thighs

Ruled by the expansive and optimistic planet Jupiter, Sagittarius is the adventurer of the Zodiac par excellence. The symbol for Sagittarius has changed greatly over time. Once the symbol was a centaur with a bow and arrow. Now only the arrow and a fragment of the bow are usually drawn. People born under the sign of Sagittarius are open, gregarious and freedom-loving in the extreme. They love to broaden their horizons constantly through travel or study. Hating to be confined by anything or anyone, Sagittarius is often more fulfilled by the journey they take rather than the destination they reach. Their openness and sense of fun makes them attractive to others and various adventures are sure to follow! However, marriage may be less appealing if the Sagittarian feels their freedom will be compromised. Truth and justice are very important to deep-thinking Sagittarians who value honesty highly. Even so, they must be careful not to allow their ideas to become too abstract and academic. Sagittarians can seem opinionated or even fanatical if their own pet theories fly in the face of common sense – they do not make great diplomats. They speak their mind as directly as possible and this will ruffle a few feathers from time to time. But the honesty and idealism of Sagittarians ensures they are always well liked.

CAPRICORN

DATES:	December 22nd–January 19th
TEMPERAMENT:	Introvert
RULING PLANET:	Saturn
ELEMENT:	Earth
QUALITY:	Cardinal
AREA OF THE BODY:	Bones and knees

Ruled by the conservative and contentious planet Saturn, Capricorn is primarily concerned with what can be achieved over the long-term. The symbol for Capricorn is one of the most obscure in the Zodiac, but is now generally drawn as the mountain goat. This represents ambition and endurance as this goat can scale great and rocky heights to reach the summit of material success where others often fail. However, the mountain top with its panoramic views is also a place of spiritual meditation. Those born under the sign of Capricorn are solidly determined to make their mark in the world and will work consistently to achieve the worldly status and wealth they crave so much. They feel a constant need to improve themselves and are determined to reach the top of their professions even if this means manoeuvring the opposition out of the way to get there. Despite their somewhat austere demeanour, Capricorns do have a great sense of humour – albeit a rather dry one – which emerges when Capricorns feel secure enough to let their hair down. Though fiercely independent, Capricorns want to be married because they have a firm belief in the benefits of following tradition. It is through this conservative approach to life that Capricorns are able to gain support for their personal ambitions since they fit in with existing power structures rather than threatening them.

Below: Capricorns are determined to reach the top of their professions even if this means manoeuvring the opposition out of the way to get there.

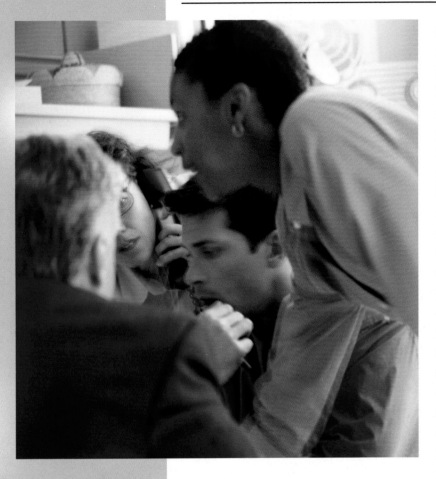

Above: Aquarians function best when engaged in group-orientated projects, preferably those that will benefit others as well as themselves.

Aquarius

DATES:	January 20th–February 18th
TEMPERAMENT:	Extrovert
RULING PLANET:	Uranus/Saturn
ELEMENT:	Air
QUALITY:	Fixed
AREA OF THE BODY:	Ankles and lower legs

The symbol for Aquarius is of a woman carrying a pitcher of water who then disperses this life-giving elixir for the good of humanity. Those born under this unusual and highly independent sign are true humanitarians who insist on seeing everyone as equal, and hate affectation and deceit of any kind. Aquarius is ruled by the eccentric and non-conformist planet Uranus, which refuses to follow the pattern of the other planets. The Aquarian person then is always uniquely original in everything they do. They love company and are very popular despite being somewhat detached and impersonal in their dealing with others. This is because Aquarians are always ready to make friends with anybody, regardless of background and status, and are solidly loyal to those they love. This, however, is where the Aquarian consistency ends. They can be perversely inconsistent, stubborn and rebellious in the extreme. Aquarians will not tolerate any kind of restriction and can become very difficult to handle if they feel their freedom is being compromised. Although Aquarians can give the appearance of calmness, they do in fact have very nervous constitutions and anxiety can make them ill, especially in the stomach area. Aquarians function best when engaged in group-orientated projects, preferably those that will benefit others as well as themselves. Here they are tireless workers who can be relied upon to add a unique spark of ingenuity to any task.

PISCES

DATES:	February 19th–March 20th
TEMPERAMENT:	Introvert
RULING PLANET:	Neptune/Jupiter
ELEMENT:	Water
QUALITY:	Mutable
AREA OF THE BODY:	Feet

Pisces is the last sign of the Zodiac and completes the circle back to Aries. Whereas Aries was brash and aggressive, Pisces is extremely sensitive and compassionate. The symbol for Pisces is of two fishes trying to swim in opposite directions but bound together by a thread. This is reflected in the personality of the Pisces-born person who can never quite decide which way to go. Though well-meaning, Pisceans do not have much willpower and are easily swayed by others. They hate to say no to anyone because they are endlessly sympathetic and feel other people's pain deeply.

Pisceans are very self-sacrificing and capable of real unconditional love. Though not materialistic, Pisceans can seem penny-pinching when they are young. This is because they constantly worry about life getting out of control. If they can develop a simple faith in the positive outcome of events, Pisceans can use their mystical intuition to great creative effect. When not acting efficiently, life to Pisceans can feel like a strange dream where nothing actually gets done. They seem to be perpetually exhausted by the rigours of everyday life. Any involvement with a Piscean is sure to be a loving and sensitive experience although more pragmatic people may become irritated by the Piscean's other-worldly perspective on reality and fatalistic approach to life.

Below: any involvement with a Piscean is sure to be a loving and sensitive experience.

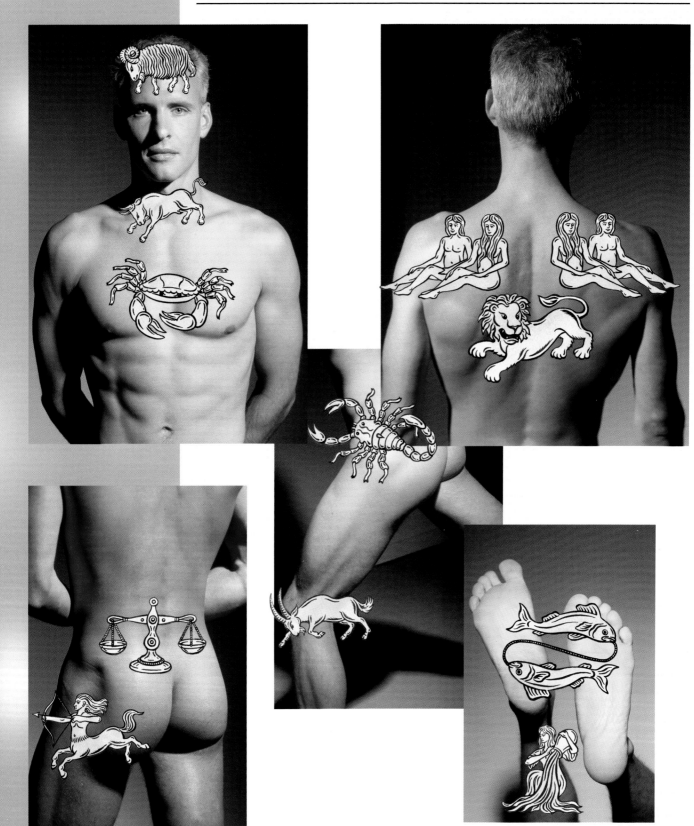

PARTS OF THE BODY

Each of the 12 Zodiac signs has traditionally been associated with a different area of the human body. These are as follows:

ARIES –	HEAD AND BRAIN
TAURUS –	NECK AND THROAT
GEMINI –	SHOULDERS AND ARMS, LUNGS AND NERVOUS SYSTEM
CANCER –	BREASTS, CHEST AND STOMACH
LEO –	HEART AND UPPER BACK
VIRGO –	INTESTINES AND ABDOMEN
LIBRA –	KIDNEYS, LOWER BACK AND BUTTOCKS
SCORPIO –	BLADDER AND SEX ORGANS
SAGITTARIUS –	HIPS AND THIGHS
CAPRICORN –	BONES, KNEES, TEETH AND SKIN
AQUARIUS –	ANKLES AND LOWER LEGS, CIRCULATORY SYSTEM
PISCES –	FEET, LYMPHATIC SYSTEM

Far left: each of the 12 Zodiac signs has traditionally been associated with a different area of the human body.

The different streams of energy flowing from the Zodiac signs affects how the body develops and determines what the pattern of wear and tear will be. Using this system with your birth chart can help to identify which are your weak and strong areas. Start by looking at your birth Sun sign. This indicates those areas in your body most affected by the Zodiacal energies. The fact that a particular body part is associated with your Sun sign does not necessarily mean that area is weak. It may be that that area is unusually strong. The whole birth chart must be examined to determine your overall state of health, but any planet in a particular Zodiac sign at the time of birth does mean the body area associated with it is worthy of more attention.

Above: the masculine/ positive signs are essentially extrovert, aggressive and assertive. The feminine/negative signs are primarily introverted and passive in nature.

MASCULINE AND FEMININE SIGNS

There are various groupings of the Zodiac signs that help to identify their respective characteristics. One such grouping divides the signs into masculine/positive and feminine/negative categories. Each sign is either masculine or feminine. Aries is the first masculine sign. Then each sign alternates between the masculine and feminine polarities as listed below.

The masculine/positive signs are essentially extrovert, aggressive and assertive. They take the initiative in situations rather than waiting for other people or circumstances to lead the way.

The feminine signs are each alternate sign beginning with Taurus. The feminine/negative signs are primarily introverted and passive in nature. They can sometimes act aggressively, but usually wait to see how events unfold before taking action.

Masculine	Feminine
Aries	Taurus
Gemini	Cancer
Leo	Virgo
Libra	Scorpio
Sagittarius	Capricorn
Aquarius	Pisces

THE TRIPLICITIES (ELEMENTS)

Another grouping of the Zodiac signs categorises them by Elements. The four elements of Fire, Earth, Air and Water were used in the ancient world to describe the interaction, balance, harmony and chaos of the natural world. Each of the Zodiac signs is represented by one of these four elements and describes different, though basic, personality types.

FIRE –	*Aries, Leo, Sagittarius*
EARTH –	*Taurus, Virgo, Capricorn*
AIR –	*Gemini, Libra, Aquarius*
WATER –	*Cancer, Scorpio, Pisces*

All the Fire signs display leadership and initiative qualities in some way. Aries likes to be in the vanguard of new endeavours and is always first in line for anything. Leo possesses managerial prowess and likes to be the single, dramatic focus of attention. Sagittarius will take the lead in matters of philosophical thought and the ethics of any situation.

All the Earth signs show consistent practicality in some area. Taurus is adept on the physical plane and will determinedly gather money and material possessions. Virgo focuses on the practical uses of intelligence and efficiently maintains the physical body and any work that requires detail. Capricorn brings the vision and ambition to climb to the top of large business organisations and to control smaller scale projects like household budgets.

The Air signs focus on the intellect and communication in some form. Gemini is quick to see both sides of any issue and can be relied on to think of something original based on what has been learnt. Libra has the ability to balance many different viewpoints to find a harmonious consensus and keep the status quo. Aquarius has the foresight and vision to understand universal principals that can be used for the betterment of mankind.

The Water signs live in the fluid world of emotion and feeling. Cancer displays great nurturing compassion especially in home and family affairs. Scorpio possesses enormous sexual intensity and has a fascination for ultimate life and death questions. Pisces has an acute sensitivity to the environment and is strongly motivated by deep subconscious forces.

THE QUALITIES

Yet another grouping of the Zodiac signs divides them into what are known as Qualities. These are three categories based on how the signs respond to changing circumstance and how adaptable and reactive. They are:

Cardinal	Aries, Cancer, Libra, Capricorn
Fixed	Taurus, Leo, Scorpio, Aquarius
Mutable	Gemini, Virgo, Sagittarius, Pisces

All the Cardinal Zodiac signs react quickly and decisively in new situations. These signs generally take the initiative, but sometimes run roughshod over others.

All the Fixed signs display great endurance and persistence to achieve long-term goals. But these signs can lack flexibility and can be stubborn.

All the Mutable signs are very versatile and can always be relied on to think of new and ingenious ways of dealing with changing circumstance. Although resourceful, these signs can project nervousness and worry.

The individual energies of each Zodiac sign are focused on one or other of the planetary bodies in our solar system. That is why each Zodiac sign is said to be ruled by a particular planet. Each planet, and the Sun and Moon, has its own particular quality of energy based on the substances from which it is composed, its history and its own unique orbit around the Sun.

THE LUMINARIES

THE SUN

The Sun is the star at the centre of our solar system giving light and heat to all the planets surrounding it, including our own tiny Earth. The glyph for the Sun is a circle with a dot at its centre. This is a mini picture of the solar system itself. It symbolises that point of singular power inside the circle that represents the completeness of the energy flow within the solar system. The one thing almost everyone knows about their own astrology is their Sun sign. The Sun is said to travel through each of the 12 Zodiac signs during the course of a year. This does not mean the Sun is actually in those Zodiac signs since the Sun does not noticeably move at all, but rather it means the Sun appears to be in each Zodiac sign in turn when viewed from the Earth as it makes its yearly orbit around the Sun. The Sun in astrology represents each person's creative centre and sense of authority. Its position shows how each of us expresses our willpower, courage and sense of purpose.

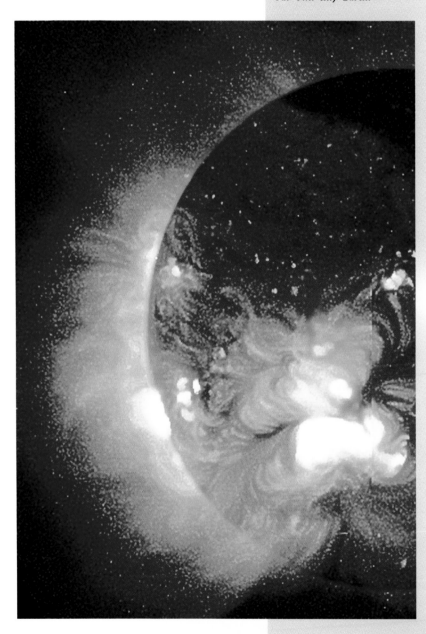

Below: the Sun is the star at the centre of our solar system giving light and heat to all the planets surrounding it, including our own tiny Earth.

THE MOON

The glyph for the Moon is the familiar waxing crescent shape, growing towards full. The Moon is a dead entity that has no internal heat and it therefore cannot radiate any life energy of its own. Rather, the Moon reflects energy from the Sun. The physical mass of the Moon does, however, move our seas and oceans about to create the tides. Once it is understood that water signifies the emotions in the language of mythology, it's clear how both our individual moods and collective, cultural attachments are strongly influenced by the Moon. In the astrological birth chart, the Moon governs our instinctive emotional responses to the environment. It stimulates those repetitive and habitual patterns of behaviour that prevent us from being as creative as the Sun would indicate.

THE INNER PLANETS

MERCURY

The glyph for Mercury is a circle with a cross dangling beneath it. The top of the circle has an upturned semi-circle attached to it, giving the appearance of ears. In mythology, Mercury was the lightning fast messenger of the gods who had wings on his helmet to symbolise the speed of communication. Mercury then represents our ability to communicate whether through talking, writing, or teaching. Mercury's placement in an astrological birth chart determines our mental frequency and how we think. Because the orbit of Mercury keeps it within a close 28 degrees of the Sun, there is always a close identification between what we think and our creative will.

Venus

Venus has always been seen as having a strong connection with the Earth because it is a similar size and distance from the Sun. The glyph for Venus is like that for Mercury but without the wings; that is to say, it consists of a circle attached to the top arm of a cross. Venus, known as the goddess Aphrodite to the ancient Greeks, has long been associated with love and attraction. Venus traditionally indicates our attitude to relationships in general and love relationships in particular. It also describes our need for beauty and harmony and determines each person's capacity for pleasure. The placement of Venus shows how the principal of attraction and repulsion operates within us on all levels. Experiencing the internal friction caused by the interplay of these opposite states in everyday life stimulates consciousness.

Mars

In contrast to the feminine planet Venus, the red planet Mars is very masculine in character. The glyph for Mars is a circle with an arrow protruding from the upper right-hand side. This one pointed arrow has a phallic quality that indicates the fiery assertiveness and aggressive strength of the Martian temperament. The placement of Mars in our birth chart determines how forceful each of us is in asserting ourselves: how we respond to fight or flight situations. This governs physical activity including the sex drive and the extreme emotions that accompany those heightened states, such as passionate desire, jealousy and violence.

JUPITER

Jupiter is that giant planet shrouded in swirling cloud that was considered the beneficent father of the gods by the ancients. The glyph for Jupiter is a cross with an upright semi-circle attached to the left arm. In astrology, Jupiter signifies growth and expansion. As well as indicating an individual's physical growth pattern and development, Jupiter also governs our potential to explore the world through study or travel. Those philosophical ideals and spiritual goals that can enrich society as well as the individual also come under the auspices of Jupiter. In this way the influence of Jupiter affects whole social movements and the rise and fall of religious and moral doctrines. Devotion to a pet cause can expand to become fanaticism under the enthusiastic influence of Jupiter.

SATURN

Saturn with its famous rings, is the farthest planet from the Sun that we can see with the naked eye. Before the discovery of the outer planets in more recent centuries, Saturn was considered to mark the outer edge of our solar system. The glyph for Saturn is almost the reverse of Jupiter's. It consists of a cross with a semi-circular arch attached to the lower arm. Whereas Jupiter in astrology represents expansion, Saturn represents contraction and limitation. The rings surrounding Saturn suggest the outer limits of what can be achieved at any point. Saturn's placement in the birth chart brings a serious and conservative discipline into our lives that can be challenging but which is necessary for us to achieve long-term goals. The delays and hardships associated with Saturn ensure the victories we win are worthy. Wisdom is achieved through patiently overcoming fear and frustration.

THE OUTER PLANETS

URANUS

Uranus was discovered in 1789 during a period of great international instability and sudden change. At this time, world changing events such as the French Revolution, the Industrial Revolution and the American War of Independence were taking place. The discovery of Uranus was a shock at the time because Saturn was previously thought to mark the limit of our solar system. The glyph for Uranus is a cross with a circle suspended from the lower arm and a semi-circle attached to each of the side arms of the cross. Uranus then brings sudden and dramatic unexpected change, often working to reform society as a whole more than on a personal level. The glyph is reminiscent of a TV aerial and indicates Uranus' resonance with electricity and innovative communication technologies such as computers.

NEPTUNE

The elusive planet Neptune was discovered in 1846 after much confusion and misinformation. Its orbit was not easy to pin down. The glyph for Neptune is a cross with an upturned semi-circle cutting through the upper arm of the cross – giving the appearance of the three-pronged trident that the sea-god Neptune carries. The mysterious and watery quality of Neptune links this planet with mystical urges and the world of psychic sensitivity. Real insights into the subconscious are possible through examining Neptune's placement in a birth chart, but nothing involving Neptune can be taken on face value. The power of the imagination is great. Illusion, deception and distortion through drugs etc. are also distractions associated with Neptune. Popular music and the movie industry are both ruled by Neptune.

Below: the tiny, cold and distant Pluto was not actually observed until 1930.

PLUTO

The glyph for Pluto consists of a cross with an upturned semi-circle balanced on the upper arm of the cross. A full circle is cradled inside the upturned semi-circle. The tiny, cold and distant Pluto was not actually observed until 1930, although the debate still continues as to whether or not it fully fits the criteria to be considered a planet at all. This ambiguity is to be expected since recent experiments into atomic matter have forced science to redefine what is real and what is theoretical.

Like its atomic namesake plutonium, Pluto in astrology deals with transformation on the most fundamental of levels – including the process of death and rebirth. Pluto brings complete change into our lives and this sometimes requires total disintegration in order to rebuild from scratch.

THE HOUSES

The Zodiac can be thought of as a great celestial wheel surrounding the Earth and divided into the 12 Zodiac signs. But inside this great Zodiac wheel is a smaller wheel that rotates in 24 hours as the result of the daily rotation of the Earth. This smaller wheel is also divided into 12 sections like the spokes of a wheel. These divisions are known as the 12 Houses and the spokes or edges of each section are called the House Cusps.

Left: the Zodiac can be thought of as a great celestial wheel surrounding the Earth and divided into the 12 Zodiac signs.

Each of the Houses from one to 12 describes a different department of life. Broadly speaking, the Houses have similar characteristics as the Zodiac signs that share the same number. For example: the first House has many of the assertive characteristics of Aries, which is the first sign. The second House shares materialistic qualities with the second sign Taurus etc. The difference is that whereas the Zodiac signs are multi-levelled in their influence, the Houses operate more on physical and practical levels. This is why they are often called the Mundane Houses.

Right: the third House indicates how you communicate with the immediate environment through conversation, phone calls, email and letters etc.

1st House

The first House indicates your sense of self-identity and self-image. It shows how you really are, in contrast to your Sun sign which shows how you project yourself to the world. The first House also gives information about your physical appearance.

2nd House

This House covers your attitude to making and spending money and how you view personal possessions. Emotional and material possessiveness are both governed by this House. Your sense of body awareness and attitude to natural resources are also found here.

Below: emotional and material possessiveness are both governed by the 2nd House.

3rd House

This House indicates how you communicate with the immediate environment through conversation, phone calls, email and letters etc. It also covers short-distance travel and your relationships with any brothers, sisters, neighbours and other people you meet on a daily basis.

4th House

Home and family issues arise here. This House indicates your basic sense of security. It governs your link with your racial, cultural and family history, psychological conditioning during childhood and relationship with parents.

5TH HOUSE

This House is primarily concerned with creative self-expression. This creativity could be artistic and leisure pursuits that you are attracted to, or it could be those procreational instincts that lead to pregnancy and the welfare of children. Love, romance and sexual desire all come under the fifth House.

6TH HOUSE

Practical work and the efficient use of time come under the auspices of this House. Routine tasks and duties and your relationship with employers and employees are found here. This House also concerns health, hygiene and dietary matters.

7TH HOUSE

Whereas the first House concerns your self, the opposite seventh House deals with your relationship with others. One-to-one encounters and close relationships of both a personal and professional nature are indicated here. All contractual matters such as marriage, divorce, legal actions and enemies are found here.

8TH HOUSE

Shared resources, joint finances tax, insurance and inheritance issues arise in the eighth House. This House is also concerned with your deeper attitudes to birth, death and rebirth. Intense emotions and sex are also covered here.

Below: one-to-one encounters and close relationships of both a personal and professional nature are indicated in the seventh House.

Above: the ninth House deals with your philosophical and religious outlook.

Right: mystical inclinations, dreams and hidden fears will all find expression in the twelfth House.

9TH HOUSE

This is an expansive House, dealing with your philosophical and religious outlook, belief system and any higher education you may pursue to arrive at these beliefs. Long-distance travel and contact with foreign cultures also arises here along with publicity and advertising.

10TH HOUSE

Where the fourth House dealt with home and family matters, its opposite House, the tenth, is concerned with what you can achieve in your own right. This House indicates your career, public role and status in the world at large. Your attitude to authority is also found here.

11TH HOUSE

This House shows how you are able to get along with others as part of a group and how altruistic you are in your outlook. Personal contacts, friendships and your involvement with humanitarian causes are indicated here.

12TH HOUSE

The subconscious mind and other psychological health matters concerning both the self and society at large are indicated in the 12th and last House. Mystical inclinations, dreams and hidden fears will all find expression here as this House deals with the legacy of the past.

CHART CALCULATION

REQUIRED INFORMATION

Your astrological birth chart is known as your Natal Chart. This chart is drawn up using your time, date and place of birth and freezes the planetary positions as seen from the Earth at your moment of birth. Since even identical twins are born at least a few minutes apart, your Natal Chart is unique to you and you alone. It is your basic blueprint showing the physical, emotional and mental equipment that you must work with during your life. It also indicates your potential for spiritual development. The calculations needed to draw up your Natal Chart are not difficult, but some of them are a little fiddly! However, once the chart is drawn, you can keep it to refer to throughout your life since this chart does not change over time.

In order to draw up an accurate Natal Chart, you need to know the date and year you were born and your birth time as accurately as possible. Then you must look up the longitude and latitude of your place of birth and convert the local birth time to GMT or Greenwich Mean Time. Some people may not know their exact birth time.

But, whilst you may not discover some details such as the correct Ascendant or House Cusps, the

planetary positions do not change much during the course of one day so you can still draw up a worthwhile chart!

Above: your astrological birth chart is drawn up using your time, date and place of birth and freezes the planetary positions as seen from the Earth at your moment of birth.

NECESSARY REFERENCE MATERIAL

There are several books that are essential to help you draw your Natal Chart:

• A planetary ephemeris for your particular birth year — such as Raphael's Ephemeris.

• A good atlas such as The Times Atlas to look up the longitude and latitude of your place of birth.

• A table of Houses such as Raphael's Table of Houses in Northern Latitudes or Raphael's Table of Houses in Great Britain. This provides the House Cusp and Ascendant information.

• Time change information concerning time zones and summertime changes can be found in Doris Doane's Time Changes in the World.

FINDING YOUR ASCENDANT, HOUSE CUSPS AND PLANETARY POSITIONS

1 You must first convert your birth time to GMT or Greenwich Mean Time. Look up your place of birth in Time Changes in the World to find any local time changes.
For example, if you were born in England during British summertime, you will have to subtract one hour from the birth time to get the GMT time.

Outside of Britain you will also need to subtract or add the appropriate number of hours for that time zone to convert the birth time to GMT. For example, Los Angeles might be PST or Pacific Standard Time. If Los Angeles is eight hours west of Greenwich, eight hours must be subtracted to get the GMT birth time. If the time zone is East of Greenwich, then you must add the appropriate hours.

2 Look up the sidereal time for your birth date in the ephemeris. This is the time at Greenwich at noon (or midnight depending on your ephemeris).

3 Now work out the difference between your GMT birth time and the sidereal time in the ephemeris. If your birth time was before noon, subtract the difference.
If your birth time was after noon, then you add the difference.

4 Now you must correct the sidereal time. The formula is 10 seconds for each hour of difference between the GMT birth time and noon. So, if you were born at 8.45am (4 hours and 15 minutes before noon), the calculation would be 10sec X 4 and one quarter = 43sec. As before, you subtract if the birth time was before noon and add if it was after noon.

5 Look up the longitude of your place of birth in the atlas.

6 Correct the longitude by multiplying the degrees and minutes of longitude by four. Take the result as minutes and seconds of time. For example, if you were born 4 degrees 11 minutes west, multiply this by four to get 16 minutes 44 seconds. Remember to subtract if west of Greenwich and add if east of Greenwich. You will arrive at your final sidereal birth time accurate to one second.

You can add or subtract 24 hours at any point in these calculations in order to keep the result a positive number between 0 and 24 hours.

Above: you must first convert your birth time to GMT or Greenwich Mean Time.

7 You can now convert your sidereal birth time into the Ascendant and House Cusps. Look up the latitude of the place you were born in the atlas. Then find the table for the nearest latitude in the Table of Houses book.

Above: if you were born at 8.45am (4 hours and 15 minutes before noon), the calculation would be 10sec X 4 and one quarter = 43sec. You subtract if the birth time was before noon and add if it was after noon.

8 The left-hand column of each table is headed 'Sidereal time'. This column lists hours (hrs), minutes (m) and sometimes seconds (s). The following columns show the House Cusps and Ascendant for that time. Find the row with the closest match to your own sidereal birth time. Look also at the sidereal time of the rows immediately above and below the best match. You will see how the Ascendant and House Cusps change incrementally every few minutes. It is then easy to see what the

Ascendant and House Cusps are for your exact sidereal birth time. You only need half the House Cusps to know them all since the 4th House Cusp is directly opposite the 10th etc.

If you were born in the southern hemisphere, simply add 12 hours to the sidereal birth time and reverse the Zodiac signs of the House Cusps listed in the table of Houses. For example, a Gemini Ascendant would become Sagittarius.

Now you have all the House Cusps and the Ascendant for your chart.

9 You can look up the planetary positions by again finding your birth date in the ephemeris. The columns show each planet's sign and degree for each day. Remember to look at the day before and after your birth date to help refine the planetary positions. For instance, the Sun moves about one degree per day. If you were born around midnight for instance, you would list your Sun position as about midway between the listed positions for the previous day and the next. Only the Moon moves significantly every day since it travels roughly one half of a degree per hour.

You now have all your planetary positions, House Cusps and your Ascendant and are ready to transfer this information onto a chart wheel.

DRAWING THE CHART WHEEL

You can buy blank birth chart wheels that you can easily draw your own planetary data onto, but it is not difficult to draw your own from scratch.

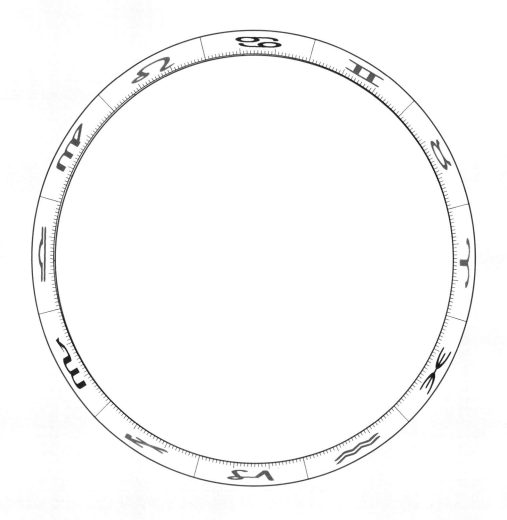

Left: divide the area between these two concentric circles into 12 equal parts each one 30 degrees long. These are the Zodiac signs so draw them in from Aries through to Pisces in an anti-clockwise direction.

1 First draw a circle about 6 inches across.

2 Then draw another circle inside the first but about one centimetre smaller all round.

3 Divide the area between these two concentric circles into 12 equal parts each one 30 degrees long. These are the Zodiac signs so draw them in from Aries through to Pisces in an anti-clockwise direction. You now have a circular band of Zodiac signs with a large blank circle in the middle in which to draw the House Cusps and planets etc.

Below: each Zodiac sign is 30 degrees long so it is easy to draw in the House Cusp lines as listed in the table of Houses.

4 Each Zodiac sign is 30 degrees long so it is easy to draw in the House Cusp lines as listed in the table of Houses. Remember that each line runs through the centre of the wheel to reach the same degree of the opposite Zodiac sign. Start by drawing in the Ascendant line. For example, if your Ascendant is 21 degrees Scorpio, draw a line from this point through the centre to 21 degrees Taurus, which is the seventh House Cusp. The other House Cusps can be drawn in a similar way. Like the Zodiac signs, the Houses follow an anti-clockwise direction from House 1, which is the Ascendant, through to House 12.

5 Once all the House Cusps are drawn in, you can draw in the Sun, Moon and each planet. Each planet will then be in a particular Zodiac sign and House.

6 You can now work out the relationships known as aspects between the Sun and Moon, the planets, the Ascendant (first House Cusp) and the MC (tenth House Cusp).

If any of these points are at the same degree of any Zodiac sign, there is a good chance that there is what is known as an aspect between them. The main aspects are as follows:

Conjunction	0 degrees apart
Sextile	60
Square	90
Trine	120
Inconjunct	150
Opposition	180

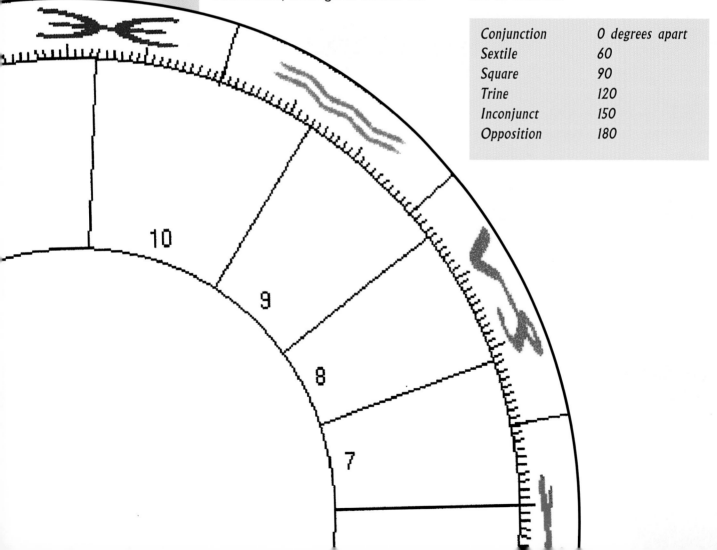

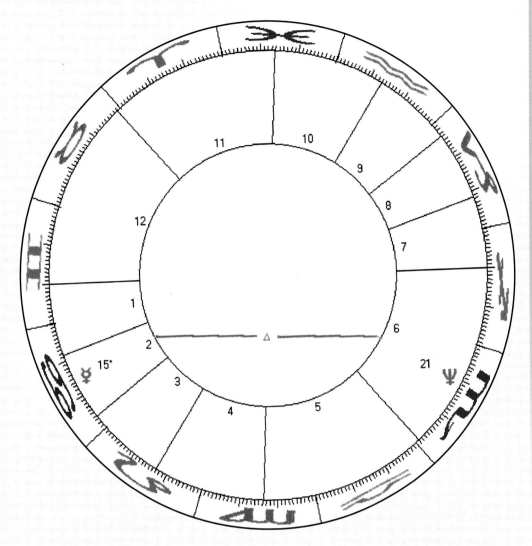

Left: if Mercury is at 15 degrees of Cancer and Neptune is at 21 degrees of Scorpio, then there is a Trine aspect between them. Therefore, a line should be drawn connecting Mercury and Neptune. It may be useful to draw the aspects in different colours to make them easier to identify afterwards.

A tolerance or leeway of 8 degrees is generally given for each aspect. For example, if Mercury is at 15 degrees of Cancer and Neptune is at 21 degrees of Scorpio, then there is a Trine aspect between them. Therefore, a line should be drawn connecting Mercury and Neptune. It may be useful to draw the aspects in different colours to make them easier to identify afterwards.

If you find drawing your Natal Birth Chart too difficult, there are many companies on the internet that can do the calculations for you.

INTERPRETING THE CHART

PLANETS IN SIGNS

Below: the Moon and each of the planets are also in one particular Zodiac sign or another in your birth chart at the time of your birth.

The one thing most people know about their own birth chart is their Sun sign. This is what people mean when they ask, 'What sign are you?' This does not mean the Sun was actually located in that particular Zodiac sign – the Sun does not noticeably move at all. Rather, it means the Sun appeared to be in that constellation when viewed from our orbiting Earth at the time you were born. In the same way that the Sun is said to be in a particular sign, the Moon and each of the planets are also in one particular Zodiac sign or another in your birth chart at the time of your birth.

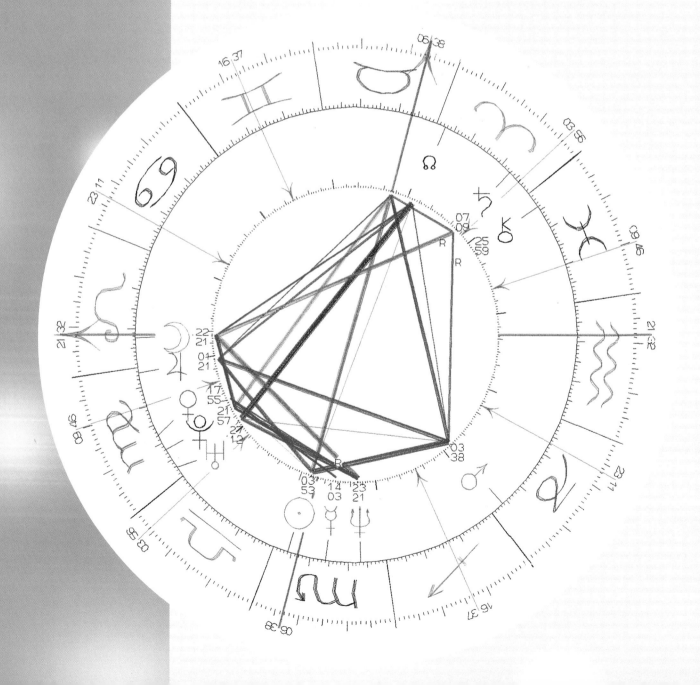

When you come to interpreting your chart, read the chapter describing the various constellations to find out about your Sun sign. This chapter can also be used to find the basic characteristics of your Ascendant sign.

When you want to discover what each planet will signify in a particular Zodiac sign, read the appropriate section that describes each planet in the chapter about planets. Then cross reference that information with the appropriate Zodiac sign in the chapter about Zodiac signs. This will show how the energy from that particular planet is modified by the sign it is in.

PLANETS IN HOUSES

Each of the Houses from one to 12 describes a different department of life. Every planet in an individual's birth chart is located in a particular House as well as in a particular Zodiac sign. This means that the energies radiating from any planet are experienced by the individual in that area of life governed by the House the planet is in. For example, if your birth chart has Mars in the second House, you are likely to be aggressive and passionate in the pursuit of money and possessions.

You should have already examined the Sun, Moon and each of the planets in a particular Zodiac sign. This will have shown how each planetary body acts in your chart. Now you can determine which area of life that planet will influence most.

Above: if your birth chart has Mars in the second House, you are likely to be aggressive and passionate in the pursuit of money and possessions.

As before, start with the Sun and look at which House the Sun is in. Then look up that House in the chapter about Houses. This will show which area of life is your main focus of attention – money, relationships, home or whatever. Remember that the Sun in your chart by sign and by House will in itself give much of the information required to understand your general life direction.

You can then gain valuable additional information by looking up the House position for the Moon and each of the planets. If, for example, the Moon is in the seventh House, your personal relationships will be very much influenced by habitual emotional patterns and perhaps by your relationship with your mother. The Zodiac sign shows how the planets act; the House indicates where they act.

Below: if the moon is in the seventh House, your personal relationships will be very much influenced by habitual emotional patterns and perhaps by your relationship with your mother.

THE ANGLES – THE ASCENDANT AND MIDHEAVEN (MC)

While all the Houses are important, those on the Angles are considered the most significant. The angular Houses are:

1st House
4th House
7th House
10th House.

The first House Cusp is called the Ascendant or rising sign. This is the exact degree of the Zodiac sign that was rising over the eastern horizon at the time and place you were born. Its opposite House, the seventh, is known as the Descendant. This is the opposite sign on the western horizon. The tenth House Cusp is called the Midheaven. This is often referred to by its Latin name meridian coeli, which is usually abbreviated to MC. This tenth House Cusp is the point directly overhead at your birth time. Its opposite point, the fourth House Cusp, is called the Nadir or immeum coeli (IC) in Latin. The fourth House Cusp is the lowest point below your feet. These four Angles and the other House Cusps can only be calculated if an accurate birth time is known.

The Ascendant (rising sign), or first House Cusp, is the most significant of the four Angles. In fact, your Ascendant sign is as important as your Sun sign in chart interpretation. Your Sun sign relates to the same month period every year. Anyone born during this month-long period would naturally share the same Sun sign as yours. However, the Ascendant sign changes every three hours because it is time and place specific. Therefore your Ascendant sign is more personal to you than your Sun sign is. It is often said by astrologers that the Sun sign indicates your true self while the Ascendant shows how you present yourself to the world at large. But, though it's certainly true that the Ascendant provides information about your physical appearance, it also relates to your basic sense of self-image.

The Ascendant is therefore critical in understanding who you really are. However, some people are more prepared to reveal their true self than others. It's easier to be expressive through your Sun sign because the personality can be used as a tool to project whatever you like in the same way that you can put on different clothes for different purposes. The more mature you are as a person, the more you are willing to express the creative potential of your Ascendant sign.

The opposite point to the Ascendant is the Descendant, or seventh House Cusp. Just as the first House concerns the self, the Descendant sign highlights what you want from other people. In other words, the Descendant indicates what you are seeking both in love relationships and in close partnerships in general.

Above: ascendant provides information about your physical appearance, it also relates to your basic sense of self-image.

Above: the Nadir relates to the more private side of your life – home, family, sense of belonging.

The Midheaven or MC on the tenth House Cusp indicates your potential for making your mark in the world. The Zodiac sign on this point is a significant indicator for determining the type of career that would suit you and the worldly status you can hope to achieve.

The opposite point to the Midheaven is the Nadir on the fourth House Cusp. Where the tenth House indicates your public life, the sign on the Nadir relates to the more private side of your life. Your attitude to home and family are explored there, as is your sense of belonging.

PLANETARY ASPECTS

The aspects play a vital part in interpreting the Natal Birth Chart. They are formed when either two planets or one planet and the Ascendant or MC are at a critical angle to each other. Astrologers use many different aspects in interpreting birth charts, but we need only deal with the major planetary aspects here. These are listed below. Remember that each aspect can be given a leeway or orb of 8 degrees on either side of the exact degree.

CONJUNCTION (0 DEGREES)

This is a powerful combination of the two planetary points concerned. Here the energies of both planets (or a planet and Ascendant or MC) fuse together in either a flowing or challenging way according to the sign and House position.

SEXTILES (60 DEGREES)

The energies of both points flow well together with creative results. This indicates an internal harmony within the person concerned in the areas governed by both points. This energy can be channelled into creative self-expression.

SQUARES (90 DEGREES)

Here, the two planetary points concerned clash. This leads to frustration in the areas governed by both points that requires perseverance and patience to overcome. On the positive side, Squares provide the impetus for self-development and the ambition to succeed in the face of conflict. Successful politicians often have many Squares in their Natal Chart.

TRINES (120 DEGREES)

Trines are generally considered to be positive aspects since the energies of the two points concerned blend well together and easily focus outward as creative self-expression. On the negative side, these planetary energies can flow so smoothly that there is little drive to improve situations and laziness can set in.

INCONJUNCTS (150 DEGREES)

An Inconjunct is technically a minor aspect and is therefore usually given a smaller orb (about 5 degrees). However, the effects of this aspect are powerful enough to be considered here. An Inconjunct gives rise to repeated inconvenient circumstances in the areas governed by the planets concerned, requiring great skill and determination to overcome.

OPPOSITIONS (180 DEGREES)

Here the planets concerned are diametrically opposed. This is a challenging situation although not necessarily as painful as the Squares aspect. The Squares produce internalised frustrations that are hard to pinpoint, whereas in the Oppositions, the differences between the planetary points are so apparent that a balance can more easily be maintained.

Below: with Conjunction the energies of both planets fuse together in either a flowing or challenging way according to the sign and House position.

ASPECTS BETWEEN PLANETS

The following section provides short descriptions of how the aspects operate with different planetary combinations. The harmonious aspects include the Sextiles and Trines. The stressful aspects include the Squares, Oppositions and Inconjuncts. The Conjunction is a generally harmonious aspect although this powerful combination of energies is sometimes considered stressful if the planets concerned have incompatible natures.

Below: Sun – Mercury aspect. Original ideas and communications are backed up with considerable force of will.

SUN – MOON

These aspects concern how the subconscious mind integrates and communicates with the conscious will. Harmonious aspects create a fusion between the emotions and the will to produce a sense of inner peace. With stressful aspects, self-expression is hindered by repetitive habit patterns.

SUN – MERCURY

Strong intellectual abilities, creativity and mental versatility are indicated here. Original ideas and communications are backed up with considerable force of will. However, a lack of objectivity or even periodic mental blind spots sometimes get the individual into trouble.

Above: the Sun – Venus aspect endows graceful charm and makes the individual an ardent lover of life.

SUN – MARS

Individuals with these aspects have considerable willpower and the courage to carry projects through. They have abundant energy and vitality along with a powerful sex drive. The stressful aspects indicate too much aggression and arguments are prone to becoming over heated.

SUN – JUPITER

An open and optimistic approach to life is indicated here. The individual with these aspects is generous and likes to help others whenever possible. Those individuals with the stressful aspects must guard against becoming too extravagant and ostentatious in dealings with others.

SUN – SATURN

All aspects involving Saturn produce limitation and restriction in some area of life. But the creativity of the Sun here means real achievements are possible if the individual is prepared to work responsibly with patience and dedication. The stressful aspects point to difficult lessons to be learned.

SUN – VENUS

This aspect suggests graceful charm and makes the individual an ardent lover of life. The emotions are strong and love and sex is usually a high priority. They can express the sort of friendly warmth that spreads goodwill. However, they can have a somewhat indulgent and narcissistic streak. Artistic or musical talents are likely.

SUN – URANUS

Individuals with these aspects will be unpredictable and even eccentric. They tend to act suddenly and without warning because their mind works in an original and inventive way. Freedom is a high priority and they love varied company. The stressful aspects suggest unreliability.

SUN – NEPTUNE

These aspects indicate an other-worldly or dream-like quality. Acute sensitivity and a high level of impressionability are usually present. Individuals with these aspects often have mystical inclinations that may be either profound or self-deceptive. The stressful aspects suggest addictive tendencies.

SUN – PLUTO

Constant self-regeneration and renewal are indicated by these aspects. These individuals often have power complexes and must guard against the tendency to dominate others. The stressful aspects suggest the temptation to dominate and aggressive behaviour toward the opposite sex.

SUN – ASCENDANT

The harmonious aspects point to powerful individuals who are really 'being themselves'. They are able to harness their creative life energy and channel that into whatever activity they choose. With stressful aspects, it is hard for these individuals to project their true selves.

Below: individuals with Sun – Uranus aspects will be unpredictable and even eccentric.

SUN – MIDHEAVEN

Individuals with these aspects can reach high positions in their chosen career and have a far-reaching influence on others. Stressful aspects indicate difficulties in dealing with authority and problems relating to employers and employees.

MOON – MERCURY

These aspects signify a direct link between the thought process and the subconscious mind. Those with the harmonious aspects are able to reason through and communicate their feelings to others. The stressful aspects suggest irrational feelings and desires.

Below: people with Moon – Venus aspects are aesthetically sensitive and artistic.

MOON – VENUS

People with these aspects are aesthetically sensitive and artistic. They make great efforts to beautify themselves and tactfully make others feel at ease. They are often good cooks and decorators. Individuals with the stressful aspects may be too submissive and accommodating which irritates others.

MOON – MARS

Assertive Mars gives power and force to the emotions. Individuals with these aspects are usually sensitive but not reticent about demonstrating their sensitivity. The harmonious aspects indicate much accomplishment, but the stressful aspects signify jealousy and outbursts of frustration or anger.

MOON – JUPITER

Individuals with these aspects are warm and generous people who love travel and adventure. They usually have an honest, optimistic approach and an ability to enjoy life. The more stressful aspects indicate over-indulgence and the pursuit of pleasure.

MOON – SATURN

These aspects can have a somewhat depressive effect. People with these aspects can be rather sombre and serious although they can display a lot of common sense. Their emotional responses are often blocked or inhibited by childhood experiences that trap them in past memories that are no longer relevant.

Above: Moon – Jupiter people are warm and generous people who love travel and adventure.

Below: people with Moon – Ascendant aspects tend to have round faces. They are very impressionable and imaginative and are emotionally attached to childhood experiences.

MOON – URANUS

Individuals with these aspects have electrically charged and erratic emotional responses. They are unpredictable, impulsive and prone to sudden changes of mood. The harmonious aspects make for popular types who are always entertaining and honest. The stressful aspects indicate irritability and unreliability.

MOON – NEPTUNE

These aspects suggest someone particularly sensitive and creative in a very mystical or psychic way. Their vivid and inspired imaginations can be used to great artistic effect. The harmonious aspects point to real spiritual aspiration and a sympathetic love of humanity. The stressful aspects indicate fantasy and deception.

MOON – PLUTO

These aspects reflect a strong psychic sensitivity and depth of feeling. Individuals with these aspects exert a subtle but powerful influence over their surroundings. The harmonious aspects signify penetrating insights into reality. The stressful aspects indicate destructive endings and emotional manipulation.

MOON – ASCENDANT

People with these aspects tend to have round faces. They are very impressionable and imaginative and are emotionally attached to childhood experiences. The stressful aspects can make the individuals concerned awkward in expressing their feelings to others.

MOON – MIDHEAVEN

The harmonious aspects point to the popularity of the people concerned. They may do well in public life and have good relationships with women. The stressful aspects suggest problems relating to the individual's parents. Domestic problems are also likely.

MERCURY – VENUS

These aspects indicate a charming, outgoing manner and often a talent People with these aspects are good conversationalists and natural diplomats. They are adept in social situations because they understand the dynamics of relationships.

Above: Mercury – Venus aspects indicate a charming, outgoing manner and often a talent for music and writing.

MERCURY – MARS

Individuals with these aspects have enormous mental energy and a skill for gathering information quickly. They can become great speech-makers and politicians. Their sharp minds are not necessarily unbiased, however. Those with the stressful aspects can be very partisan in their opinions.

MERCURY – JUPITER

People with these aspects are good communicators. They have very broad interests and are often attracted to philosophical pursuits and embrace higher education with enthusiasm. They can make good teachers and politicians. The stressful aspects indicate superfi-ciality and exaggeration.

MERCURY – SATURN

These aspects relate to great precision and agility in mental tasks. These individuals have real scientific and organizational ability because they think logically. The more stressful aspects indicate an overly cautious, fearful and somewhat stilted approach to life. Worry and pessimism must be avoided.

Mercury – Uranus

People with these aspects seem to have a streak of genius about them. They are original and inventive thinkers who are very rebellious and can be relied upon to come up with a new angle on anything. Individuals with the stressful aspects may alienate others through their eccentricities.

Mercury – Neptune

Someone with these aspects takes nothing at face value and is constantly seeking to expose some hidden agenda. Their penetrating minds make them good psychologists and investigators. Those with the stressful aspects must ensure they do not embellish reality because of mental boredom. Sometimes nothing is being hidden!

Mercury – Pluto

Individuals with these aspects have penetrating minds and are capable of perceiving the underlying patterns of behaviour that reveal hidden truths. They have something of the genius about them. They make good code-breakers and scientists. The stressful aspects indicate obsession or dictatorial behaviour.

Mercury – Ascendant

These aspects suggest a high level of intelligence and good reasoning powers. The stressful aspects suggest the individuals concerned are awkward and hesitant in expressing their thoughts to the people close to them.

Mercury – Midheaven

People with the harmonious aspects are good communicators and are able to impress those in authority with their unique ideas. Those with the stressful aspects find it hard to express their ideas in a way those in authority can appreciate.

Far left: people with Mercury – Mars aspects can become great speech-makers and politicians.

Below: people with Mercury – Pluto have something of the genius about them. They make good code-breakers and scientists.

VENUS – MARS

Here masculine desire meets feminine attraction. People with harmonious aspects are sure to be fun-loving and sensual both in sexual relationships and in general social interaction. Artistic inclinations are also likely. The stressful aspects indicate problems relating to the opposite sex or a preoccupation with sex.

VENUS – JUPITER

A cheerful, easy-going disposition is indicated by these aspects. These individuals are friendly and benevolent types who enjoy giving to those less fortunate than themselves. Those with the more stressful aspects may become somewhat extravagant and indolent.

VENUS – SATURN

Individuals with these aspects are loyal to those they love, but can take their romances too seriously – lacking a lighter touch. They often form relationships with older or more mature partners. People with the stressful aspects can be emotionally inhibited, melancholic and pessimistic about romance.

VENUS – URANUS

People with these aspects generally have intense but erratic and unpredictable relationships. Romances and friendships often begin unexpectedly under strange conditions, but can also end as suddenly as they began. The stressful aspects indicate short-lived infatuations.

Below: Venus – Jupiter; a cheerful, easy-going disposition is indicated by these aspects.

VENUS – NEPTUNE

These individuals are highly creative and sensitive types who are able to establish an almost telepathic rapport with the people they tune in to. Real spiritual love is possible here although the stressful aspects indicate deceptive and unreliable behaviour in relationships.

VENUS – PLUTO

People with these aspects frequently find themselves in passionate love relationships that can become obsessive in their intensity. There is often a sense of having known the object of their love before. Sexual desire is intense, but the stressful aspects point to jealousy or even violence.

Below: people with Venus – Pluto aspects frequently find themselves in passionate love relationships that can become obsessive in their intensity.

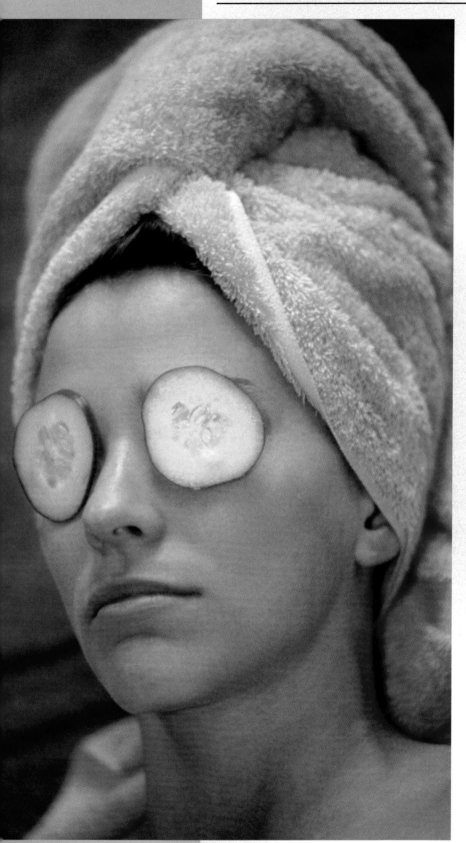

VENUS – ASCENDANT

These aspects indicate physical beauty in the individuals concerned. Other people find them attractive and appealing. Those with the stressful aspects can become obsessed with their own appearance. Emotional problems can hinder self-expression and create relationship difficulties.

VENUS – MIDHEAVEN

These individuals are socially ambitious. Those with the harmonious aspects might be successful in the arts or public relations work. People with the stressful aspects find it hard to juggle home and work responsibilities.

MARS – JUPITER

People with these aspects have enormous physical energy and drive that requires careful handling. There may be a connection with the military. Whatever they become interested in becomes a consuming preoccupation. The stressful aspects indicate fanaticism because these individuals always feel they are right.

MARS – SATURN

The individual with these aspects has a considerable capacity for hard work, courage and endurance. Unfortunately, however resourceful they are, they often seem to gain less reward for their efforts than others. The stressful aspects indicate anger, envy or even frustrated violence.

MARS – URANUS

Individuals with these aspects are likely to be impulsive and rebellious in equal measure. They fight against what they see as dull routine and often challenge the rules of society and enjoy high-risk activities. Those with the stressful aspects can be reckless to the point of courting danger.

MARS – NEPTUNE

These aspects indicate a powerful psychic aura often accompanied by strange emotional impulses and sexual desires. These people are not straightforward and act with subterfuge although they are usually attractive to others. They should be careful with drugs and alcohol since they may have addictive temperaments.

Above: Mars – Uranus aspects fight against what they see as dull routine and often challenge the rules of society and enjoy high-risk activities.

Far left: Venus – Ascendant aspects indicate physical beauty in the individuals concerned.

MARS – PLUTO

This is a particularly combustible planetary combination. Individuals with these aspects have enormous energy and willpower and would rather die than accept defeat in anything.

The sex drive, and all desires in fact, is extremely strong. People with the stressful aspects are prone to egotism, lust and greed.

MARS – ASCENDANT

These aspects indicate individuals who are aggressive and assertive in their manner of expression. They are often physically strong and muscular. The stressful aspects suggest the people concerned are overly forceful and dominating.

MARS – MIDHEAVEN

Individuals with these aspects are ambitious and are determined to reach the top of their professional tree. People with the stressful aspects may experience problems getting on with relatives and those in authority at work.

Below: individuals with Mars – Pluto aspects have enormous energy and willpower and would rather die than accept defeat in anything.

Left: Jupiter – Neptune aspects; these individuals love to feel inspired by exotic travel, music and religion.

JUPITER – SATURN

There is a clash here between the expansion of Jupiter and the contraction of Saturn. Individuals with these aspects take life seriously and work hard to achieve money and status. Many disappointments are likely – especially with the stressful aspects – but disciplined effort is eventually rewarded.

JUPITER – URANUS

People with these aspects are unconventional, but achieve their aims through unusual methods and innovation. They love to travel and their lust for life wins them many diverse friends. They prefer to work in unstructured environments. The stressful aspects indicate restlessness and frustration.

JUPITER – NEPTUNE

These individuals love to feel inspired by exotic travel, music and religion. They are imaginative and get carried away with mystical fervour. These people are compassionate and attract many strange and diverse friends, but should guard against idealism and gullibility.

JUPITER – PLUTO

Individuals with these aspects get involved in activities that will improve themselves and others, too. They may become interested in spiritual pursuits such as religion, yoga and meditation. They may also have healing abilities. People with the stressful aspects should not promise more than they can deliver.

JUPITER – ASCENDANT

People with these aspects tend to be optimistic and good-natured. They are often interested in exploring religious and philosophical ideas. Those with the stressful aspects may seem self-righteous and opinionated to other people.

JUPITER – MIDHEAVEN

Those with the harmonious aspects experience good fortune in their lives. Their honesty and generosity make others want to help them. The stressful aspects suggest ostentation and extravagance.

SATURN – URANUS

This is generally a good combination of planets because the original Uranus is able to prevent traditional Saturn from getting stuck in a rut. People with these aspects can achieve much by giving traditional ideas and methods an original twist. The stressful aspects indicate individuals who are stubborn and unrealistic.

Below: Jupiter – Ascendant; people with these aspects tend to be optimistic and good-natured.

SATURN – NEPTUNE

These aspects suggest a somewhat depressive quality. Individuals with these aspects can demonstrate great maturity and focus while still maintaining an idealistic stance. This can lead to profundity. The more stressful aspects indicate anxiety and a morbid fixation on negative thoughts.

SATURN – PLUTO

People with these aspects can have a transforming effect on the world around them. They are able to use focus and discipline to make great scientific advances. This requires much hard toil, but ambition carries them through. The stressful aspects indicate cruelty and oppression.

SATURN – ASCENDANT

Individuals with these aspects tend to be serious and austere who may appear unfriendly or unapproachable to others. The harmonious aspects indicate a good sense of responsibility. The stressful aspects suggest the individuals concerned are cold and unresponsive.

SATURN – MIDHEAVEN

People with these aspects work long and hard to achieve long-term goals and ambitions. Individuals with the stressful aspects may get embroiled in scandal and lose their advantage.

Above: individuals with Saturn – Ascendant aspects tend to be serious and austere individuals who may appear unfriendly or unapproachable to others.

Above: Uranus – Neptune; aspects between these slow moving planets tend to affect whole generations of people at once more than individuals.

URANUS – NEPTUNE

Aspects between these slow moving planets tend to affect whole generations of people at once more than individuals. The general effect is to awaken society at large to greater psychic awareness, leading to breakthroughs in understanding. The stressful aspects indicate painful shattering of widely held illusions.

URANUS – PLUTO

The general effect of this combination is to drastically reform society through implementing new technologies and ideals.
The stressful aspects suggest social unrest.

URANUS – ASCENDANT

Individuals with these aspects can be strikingly unusual in their appearance. They are often very tall. They are mentally sharp and original in their thinking. The stressful aspects suggest unreliability and individuals can be socially out of step with others.

URANUS – MIDHEAVEN

People with these aspects have unusual professions and approach work in an individualistic way. The stressful aspects indicate individuals so rebellious and non-conformist that no-one can work with them.

NEPTUNE – PLUTO

The general effect of this combination is to raise the consciousness of the population at large as subconscious barriers are removed. The stressful aspects can indicate a disintegration of society.

NEPTUNE – ASCENDANT

Individuals with these aspects often have a strange hypnotic power of attraction and seem other-worldly in some way. The stressful aspects suggest deception and ineptitude in social and romantic relationships.

NEPTUNE – MIDHEAVEN

Individuals with these aspects need to be in an artistic or creative profession where they can use their boundless imaginations. The stressful aspects indicate confusion and chaos in both work and domestic arrangements.

PLUTO – ASCENDANT

These aspects point to enormous willpower and penetrating insights into reality that go beyond normal intuition. They can become too dominating and aggressive in close relationships.

PLUTO – MIDHEAVEN

Whatever people with these aspects do in home or work life, they are sure to make an impact and may well rise to high-profile positions. The stressful aspects indicate power struggles with those in authority.

Left: Neptune – Midheaven need to be in an artistic or creative profession where they can use their boundless imaginations

ASTROLOGICAL RELATIONSHIPS

Below: the simplest way to work out the possibilities of a relationship is to compare your Sun sign with your potential lover's Sun sign.

Astrology can be a useful tool in helping you find your ideal love. The following section gives a brief interpretation of how the Zodiac signs interact. The simplest way of working out the possibilities of a relationship is to compare your Sun sign with your potential lover's Sun sign. But your Sun sign only dictates your public persona whereas your Ascendant reveals the real you. Your Descendant sign will show what you are looking for in a partner. You can gain more insight into a relationship by comparing your Ascendant and Descendant signs with those of your partner. Remember that your Descendant is the opposite sign to your Ascendant so, for example, if you have a Taurus Ascendant, you will have a Scorpio Descendant.

ARIES / ARIES

Always an immediate empathy, but competitive rams often clash horns. Not generally considered an ideal marriage since neither of you are consistent, but there will be plenty of passion while it lasts!

ARIES / TAURUS

A Taurus lover will refuse to be pushed around and will try to curb Aries' spontaneous and extravagant spending habits. But you both enjoy comfortable living conditions and the nice things in life. Good as friends or lovers.

ARIES / GEMINI

You two will get along like a house on fire! Aries may find Gemini talks a bit too much because Aries prefers to act on impulse first and talk later. But both essentially have fun together as each inspires the other's creative imagination.

ARIES / CANCER

A clash of styles here. Aries may appear brash and aggressive and Cancer might feel somewhat overshadowed. Aries may inadvertently hurt sensitive Cancer's feelings and Cancer will respond with passive resistance.

Below: Aries / Aries; there will be plenty of passion while it lasts!

Aries / Leo

A battle of wills between two extroverts competing for the limelight is inevitable, but it's all in good fun here. It's generally a good mix, provided both of you are sufficiently generous to take turns on the centre sage.

Aries / Virgo

Not a perfect relationship since high-speed Aries is likely to feel frustrated by Virgo's constant focus on seemingly trivial details. The patient Virgo could find Aries a bit too pushy and forceful for comfort.

Aries / Libra

Here, opposites attract as diplomatic Libra is able to smooth the ruffled feathers that irrepressible Aries often causes. This would be a great partnership for either business or pleasure!

Aries / Scorpio

This is a particularly sexy and passionate blend of energies and both signs will relish the emotional intensity. Whether this will be a long-term relationship or not is very much in the balance – if you can find any!

ARIES / SAGITTARIUS

You share a genuine urge for adventure and exploration so you can go far both emotionally and geographically. You each have the faith in the journey to make it work.

ARIES / CAPRICORN

Capricorn tends to be rather more calculating than the impulsive and childlike Aries, so expect some tension. Things may be passionate for a while, but arguments could soon follow.

Far left: the patient Virgo could find Aries a bit too pushy and forceful for comfort.

Below: Capricorn tends to be rather more calculating than the impulsive and childlike Aries, so expect some tension.

Far right: a great depth of love and understanding is possible with Taurus – Leo.

Below: Taurus – Cancer both of you can create a very comfortable and sharing environment.

ARIES / AQUARIUS

There is an unusual and sparkling quality to this relationship that gives it an enduring fascination. There is a mutual, high-speed mental rapport that means the relationship will never get bogged down!

ARIES / PISCES

This will be a tricky or difficult one to make work. The fiery force of Aries is very different to the dream-like world inhabited by Pisces. You could well unnerve each other!

TAURUS / TAURUS

This should be a sensual and pleasurable experience, if somewhat indulgent. The danger is in neither of you being willing to back down during conflicts which could create some unhappy stalemates.

TAURUS / GEMINI

Not an easy combination. Gemini is very quick-witted and analytical whereas Taurus, who is not that keen on self-analysis, prefers to live for the sensations of the moment.

TAURUS / CANCER

The both of you can create a very comfortable and sharing environment. Your differences are complementary rather than divisive, so you can make each other feel safe and supported.

TAURUS / LEO

A great depth of love and understanding is possible here. Though both of you are used to having your own way, your conflicts usually have a light-hearted edge that promotes reconciliation.

Below: Taurus – Libra have a shared vision of harmony and beauty so there is no clash of values or methods.

TAURUS / VIRGO

Not the most adventurous pairing, but you get on relatively well since you share a need for steadiness and dependability. You also both appreciate quality in life. Taurus may find Virgo a bit distant.

TAURUS / LIBRA

Both of you are very touchy-feely people so a very sensual relationship is in store. You have a shared vision of harmony and beauty so there is no clash of values or methods.

TAURUS / SCORPIO

This can be an emotionally powerful meeting of opposites with very erotic overtones. You share a love of sensuality and both have a somewhat possessive view of relationships.

TAURUS / SAGITTARIUS

Not one of the better matches as your temperaments are likely to clash. You generally understand where the other is coming from, but your approaches are so different that long-term success is uncertain.

Taurus / Capricorn

This partnership possesses all the hallmarks of one to stand the test of time. Together you can pool your resources and work at gradually improving your lifestyles.

Taurus / Aquarius

The eccentric Aquarius could be too much for a traditional and pragmatic Taurus to handle. Aquarius loves varied company whereas Taurus needs the attention of only its nearest and dearest.

Taurus / Pisces

Two vastly differing temperaments, but the combination of energies works particularly well. Both are able to give the other exactly what is needed in terms of love and support.

Gemini / Gemini

An unusual and highly charged combination! Geminis are contradictory at the best of times, so in this partnership you have not just two points of view but four. Is there enough room?

Above: with Gemini – Gemini you have not just two points of view but four. Is there enough room?

Right: a healthy and fun-loving rapport can be instantly built up with Gemini – Leo.

GEMINI / CANCER

This will be a difficult one to make a success of. Gemini loves to talk, but will not necessarily have the sensitivity to Cancer's feelings to say the right things. It will be hard to build up trust.

GEMINI / LEO

A healthy and fun-loving rapport can be instantly built up – which is a good starting point for any relationship! Leo loves to be the centre of attention and does not feel challenged by Gemini's intellectual approach.

GEMINI / VIRGO

You two certainly share an understanding, but the goals and means you have are so different that true empathy may be lacking. You can get on well sometimes, but argument will arise.

GEMINI / LIBRA

This is one of the Zodiac's better matches. Two charming and graceful Air signs are sure to find plenty of common ground. Each is willing to give the relationship their best.

GEMINI / SCORPIO

An interesting mix of energies, but one unlikely to bring long-term fulfilment. Both of you like to explore new experiences, but you may find it hard to express exactly how you feel to each other.

GEMINI / SAGITTARIUS

There certainly won't be many awkward silences in this talkative relationship! Both of you are game for a laugh together and love new experiences. In this case opposites definitely attract.

Below: Gemini – Sagittarius certainly won't have many awkward silences in this talkative relationship!

Gemini / Capricorn

There may not be sufficient common ground here for a real rapport to emerge. You may do business together, but there is something lacking emotionally which makes romance difficult.

Gemini / Aquarius

A mentally stimulating relationship, but it could be a bit cool on passion. As airy intellectuals you have a real rapport, but a lack of emotional intensity may mean you are best off as friends.

Gemini / Pisces

Gemini must think to live, but Pisces can only breathe in the waters of emotion. It will be difficult for this pair to forge sufficient understanding to make a close relationship work.

Cancer / Cancer

No difficulty understanding each other here– in fact you are almost telepathic in your dream-like empathy! That much insight into each other's psyche will also create some tensions.

Below: Gemini – Capricorn. You may do business together, but there is something lacking emotionally which makes romance difficult.

CANCER / LEO

Cancer will patiently nurture Leo through the dramatic eruptions that Leo invariably creates. But Cancer will have to impose limits on how much energy this relationship is worth.

CANCER / VIRGO

There can be stimulating episodes between you, but the relationship could descend into stagnant periods, too. If the goodwill is there, you can develop a deep connection.

CANCER / LIBRA

Somehow you hit it off immediately. After a while, though, this relationship could turn out to be a bit of a slog. Cancer will dig for the deeper levels that Libra may find intrusive.

CANCER / SCORPIO

This could be an ideal match for both of you. There is a deep emotional understanding, which you both need, mixed with a generous helping of pure sexual magnetism.

CANCER / SAGITTARIUS

A far-from-perfect combination of energies. Though the goodwill is present, it seems as though you are both speaking different languages. This may turn out to be an unbridgeable gulf.

CANCER / CAPRICORN

A harmonious combination of opposite temperaments could make for a real success here. If you apportion your roles wisely, you will have the basis for a happy home environment.

Below: Cancer – Scorpio. This could be an ideal match for both of you.

CANCER / AQUARIUS

This could easily turn into a painful experience for both of you. You are both hypersensitive to criticism and, though you try to give to each other, this is often in ways the other can't begin to appreciate.

CANCER / PISCES

A deeply passionate romance is possible here. You share an intense emotional empathy and a lust for sensual indulgences. This could actually work very well over the long term!

Above: Cancer – Aquarius. This could easily turn into a painful experience for both of you. You are both hypersensitive to criticism, and though you try to give to each other, this is often in ways the other can't begin to appreciate.

LEO / LEO

Every lion and lioness needs to be the centre of attention, so the two of you together could be a little too tempestuous and competitive for long-term compatibility. It may be easier to be friends.

LEO / VIRGO

A certain degree of tolerance can be expected, but perhaps there is not the degree of intimacy for love. You get on well as friends, but that extra spark for passion is elusive.

Below: Leo – Leo together could be a little too tempestuous and competitive for long–term compatibility. It may be easier to be friends.

LEO / LIBRA

Libra is much more diplomatic than flamboyant Leo, but these differences do not make for a clash of wills. You two can get on fine and are able to develop a fun-loving rapport.

LEO / SCORPIO

There is a strong sexual magnetism between you that could make for a very passionate, physical relationship. Long-term success depends on whether or not your egos clash.

LEO / SAGITTARIUS

The lion and the centaur are both powerful beasts, so expect your animal passions to be stimulated by this encounter. This will be an outgoing and lively relationship.

LEO / CAPRICORN

There may an immediate attraction, but making it last will be difficult. Capricorn seems distant to the open Leo and this lack of spontaneity feels somewhat weird.

Below: Leo – Scorpio. There is a strong sexual magnetism between you that could make for a very passionate, physical relationship.

Below: Virgo – Sagittarius is generally good-natured rapport is possible here even though your needs appear very different.

LEO / AQUARIUS

Not an ideal match, but loads of fun for the both of you and the people you spend time with. You both love varied, eccentric company, but Aquarius is more detached and impersonal than Leo in social groups.

LEO / PISCES

You are as different as fire and water, yet oddly, can develop a very romantic bond. Leo may find Pisces somewhat lacking in energy, but Pisces will want Leo to tone down a little!

VIRGO / VIRGO

Each Virgo has their own little way of doing things so success depends on whether your idiosyncrasies are compatible or not. Things will be very caring and sharing, but could also get a bit dull.

VIRGO / LIBRA

Not a compatible mix. Both of you possess graceful charm, but socialite Libra may be rather too flighty for the intense Virgo. Libra relies on other people whereas Virgo only trusts its own efforts.

VIRGO / SCORPIO

This one may take a little while to get off the ground, but passions could heat up intriguingly with practice! Prepare for lots of analysis and considerable sexual chemistry.

VIRGO / SAGITTARIUS

A generally good-natured rapport is possible here even though your needs appear very different. Could be a strong friendship, but will the passion last the test of time?

Left: a reasonable understanding and a shared need for practicality are both present with Virgo – Capricorn. You'd definitely make great friends and possibly even lovers!

VIRGO / CAPRICORN

A reasonable understanding and a shared need for practicality are both present here.
You'd definitely make great friends and possibly even lovers! Even so, perfectionist Virgo may find Capricorn a bit traditional.

VIRGO / AQUARIUS

This is quite a difficult combination of energies. Both signs are very mentally inclined, but your outlooks may be irreconcilably divergent. More talking than action may wear thin after a while.

Above: Libra – Sagittarius together are sure to make an effective united front in social situations as lots of light-hearted banter is in store.

VIRGO / PISCES

This pair of opposites could well be ideal for both of you. Virgo helps ground the sensitive Pisces while Pisces draws out Virgo's emotional depths. A wonderful combination for love.

LIBRA / LIBRA

There's certainly a profound empathy between the two of you. The big question, however, is whether or not you will ever get anything done with each of you being so indecisive!

LIBRA / SCORPIO

A strange combination yet, surprisingly, it works. Libra goes to enormous lengths to get on with everyone whereas Scorpio just exudes a magnetic sex appeal that attracts many.

LIBRA / SAGITTARIUS

You two together are sure to make an effective united front in social situations as lots of light-hearted banter is in store. Your energies flow together easily so long-term success is likely.

LIBRA / CAPRICORN

Probably not the most workable of situations. Hard-working Capricorn may view Libra's flighty socialising as trivial and lazy. Not enough common ground here for real rapport to grow.

LIBRA / AQUARIUS

You two fit together perfectly like a hand in a glove. Somehow you both know how to say and do the right things to make the other happy. This is an ideal match for love.

LIBRA / PISCES

There is something other-worldly yet somehow very comfortable about the way you cater for each other's needs. It is difficult to explain how you get along – you just do.

SCORPIO / SCORPIO

There could hardly be a more volatile and combustible concoction than two Scorpios together. The sexual tension between you makes the air positively crackle with excitement.

Below: Libra – Pisces is something other–worldly yet somehow very comfortable about the way you cater for each other's needs.

Above: Scorpio –
Capricorn.
Both of you are powerful
but evenly matched and
both respect the talents of
the other. Together you
can create lasting
achievements.

SCORPIO / SAGITTARIUS

Both of you are strong and
determined individuals who have
little in common. Sagittarius relies
on ideals whereas Scorpio prefers
the more direct, physical approach.

SCORPIO / CAPRICORN

You can't go wrong with this
relationship. Both of you are
powerful but evenly matched and
both respect the talents of the
other. Together you can create
lasting achievements.

Scorpio / Aquarius

There is real depth in your understanding of each other, but that doesn't mean you entirely trust each other either. Secretive Scorpio and gregarious Aquarius can make harmonious colleagues.

Scorpio / Pisces

You both inhabit the water world of emotion and have the ability to transport each other into the realm of love. Scorpio helps Pisces to face reality while Pisces teaches faith.

Sagittarius / Sagittarius

Two adventurous centaurs galloping wild and free are sure to have a memorable time. Longevity will depend on whether or not you are both prepared to be wrong sometimes.

Sagittarius / Capricorn

The best thing would be to accept early on that you don't see eye-to-eye rather than to prolong the agony of constantly trying to prove your point to each other. Only for those prepared for battle!

Left: Sagittarius – Sagittarius. Two adventurous centaurs galloping wild and free are sure to have a memorable time.

Below: Sagittarius – Aquarius are not a particularly good match. Sagittarius has the depth of thought and Aquarius has the range, even if only on the surface. Though both expansive signs, the differences may be unbridgeable.

SAGITTARIUS / AQUARIUS

Not a particularly good match. Sagittarius has the depth of thought and Aquarius has the range even if only on the surface. Though both expansive signs, the differences may be unbridgeable.

SAGITTARIUS / PISCES

Sagittarius means well, but may seem too direct and clumsy to avoid hurting the hypersensitive feelings of Pisces. But there is a certain attraction here, so love is possible.

CAPRICORN / CAPRICORN

One thing for sure is that, once committed, Capricorns will not break up without first exploring every avenue to avoid accepting failure. This could become too competitive for comfort.

CAPRICORN / AQUARIUS

Both of you look at life by taking a long-term view, but there the similarities end. Aquarius lives in the world of thought and spoken ideas whereas Capricorn is concerned with material, practical things.

CAPRICORN / PISCES

A loving and passionate time is in store when you two get together. Capricorn is able to provide the stable home environment that is vital for Pisces to feel safe and secure enough to bloom.

AQUARIUS / AQUARIUS

An unpredictable mix if there ever was! A relationship with your own Zodiac sign is not always recommended, but at least here you have finally found someone who can keep up mentally!

AQUARIUS / PISCES

Both of you can be vague and distracted, but unfortunately this doesn't put you in a similar space. Aquarius finds Pisces' dreaminess irritating and Pisces feels drained by Aquarius' constant conversation.

PISCES / PISCES

Here at last you have found someone who can truly share your fantasies and visions. You can create an enchanted world of love together as long as you don't end up just dreaming your lives away!

Above: a relationship with your own Zodiac sign is not always recommended, but at least here you have finally found someone who can keep up mentally!

INDEX

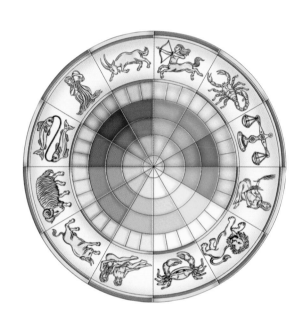